Bach
Around the Christmas Tree
18 Classic Christmas Carols in the Styles of the Great Composers

Arranged by Carol Klose

CONTENTS

ISBN 978-1-57560-458-9

Visit our website at www.cherrylane.com

Angels We Have Heard on High

In the style of Muzio Clementi

Traditional French Carol

Allegro

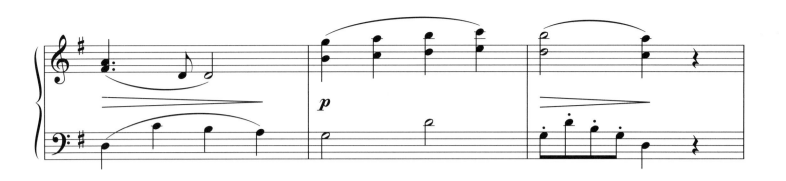

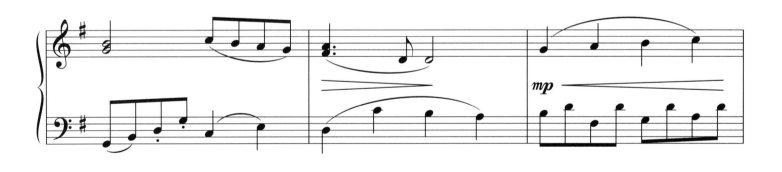

Away in a Manger

In the style of Sergei Rachmaninoff

Music by
James R. Murray

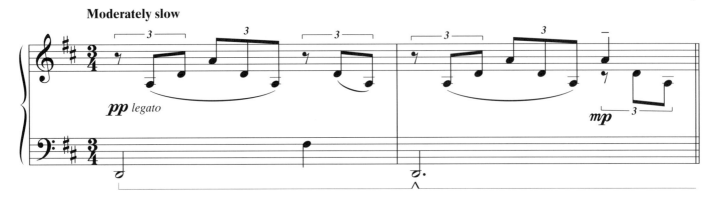

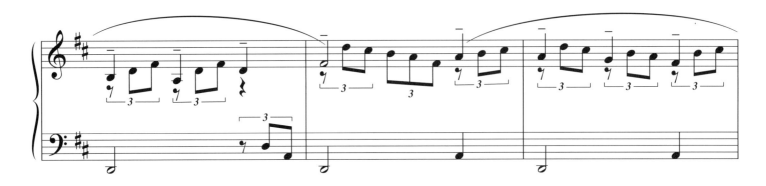

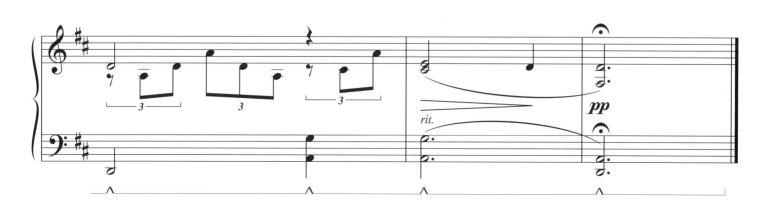

Deck the Halls
In the style of Ludwig van Beethoven

Traditional Welsh Carol

Moderately, with a crisp March feel

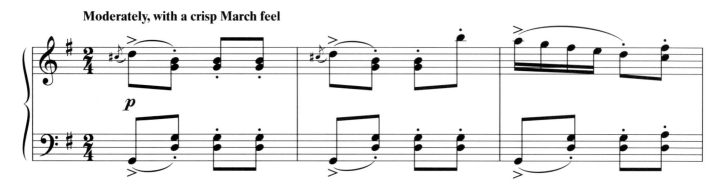

The First Noël

In the style of Johannes Brahms

17th Century English Carol
Music from *W. Sandys' Christmas Carols*

Moderate Waltz tempo

God Rest Ye Merry, Gentlemen

In the style of Ludwig van Beethoven

19th Century English Carol

Good King Wenceslas

In the style of Johann Pachelbel

Music from *Piae Cantiones*

Hark! The Herald Angels Sing

In the style of Franz Joseph Haydn

Music by Felix Mendelssohn-Bartholdy
Adapted by William H. Cummings

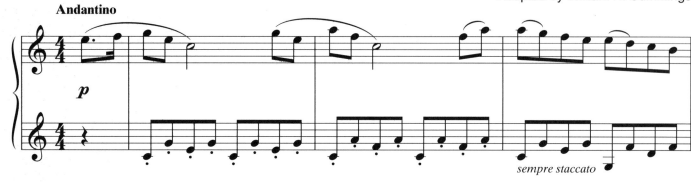

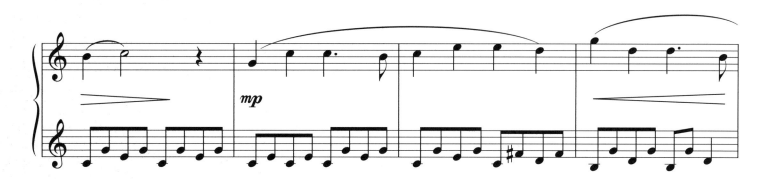

It Came Upon a Midnight Clear

In the style of Jacques Offenbach

Music by
Richard Storrs Willis

Jingle Bells

In the style of Scott Joplin

Music by
J. Pierpont

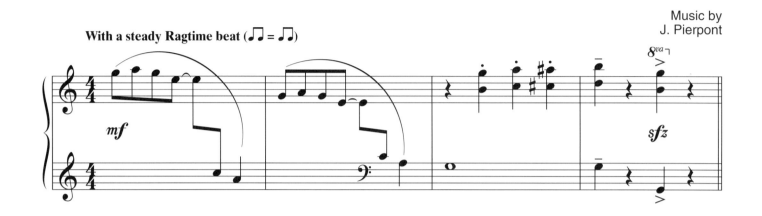

Joy to the World

In the style of George Frideric Handel

Music by George Frideric Handel
Adapted by Lowell Mason

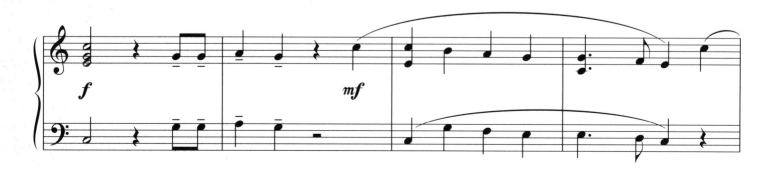

O Christmas Tree

In the style of Fryderyk Chopin

Traditional German Carol

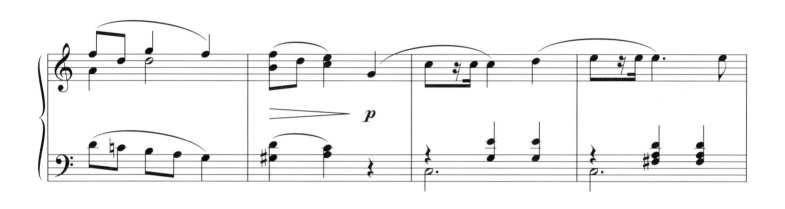

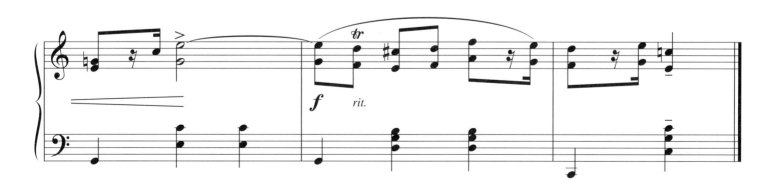

O Come, All Ye Faithful
(Adeste Fideles)
In the style of Wolfgang Amadeus Mozart

Music by
John Francis Wade

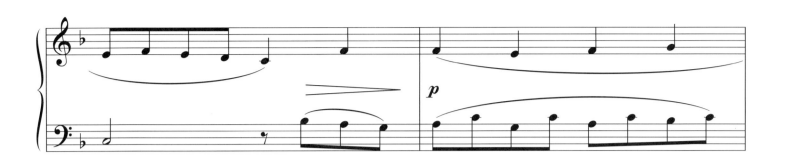

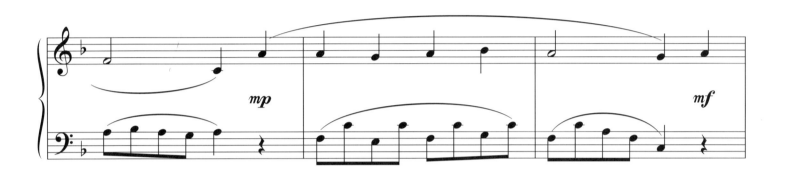

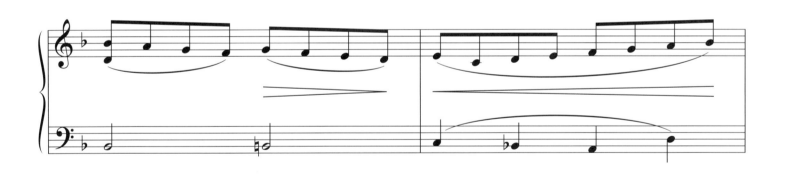

O Holy Night
In the style of Franz Schubert

Music by
Adolphe Adam

Flowing, with expression

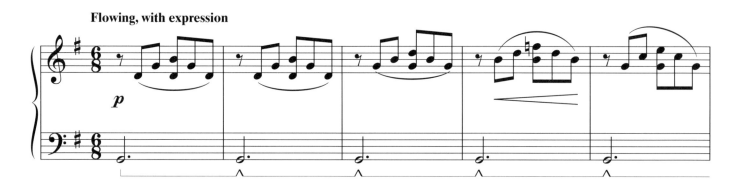

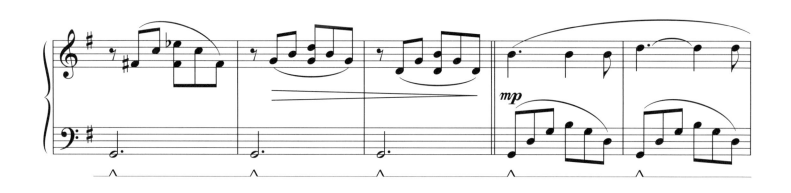

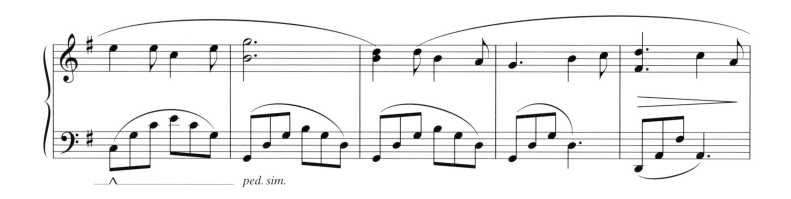

O Little Town of Bethlehem

In the style of Johann Sebastian Bach

Music by
Lewis H. Redner

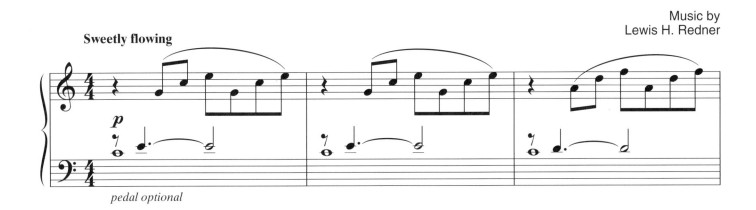

Silent Night
In the style of Johann Sebastian Bach

Music by
Franz X. Gruber

We Three Kings of Orient Are

In the style of Franz Liszt

Music by
John H. Hopkins, Jr.

We Wish You a Merry Christmas

In the style of Johann Strauss

Traditional English Folksong

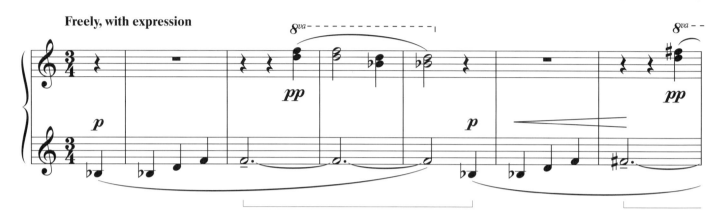

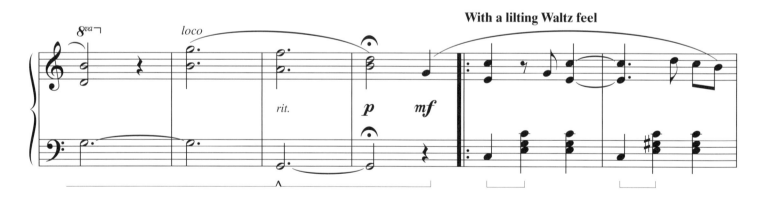

What Child Is This?

In the style of Claude Debussy

16th Century English Melody

CREATIVE PIANO SOLO

Looking to add some variety to your playing? Enjoy these beautifully distinctive arrangements for piano solo! These popular tunes get new and unique treatments for a fun and fresh presentation. Explore new styles and enjoy these favorites with a bit of a twist! Each collection includes 20 songs for the intermediate to advanced player.

BOHEMIAN RHAPSODY & OTHER EPIC SONGS

Band on the Run • A Day in the Life • Free Bird • November Rain • Piano Man • Roundabout • Stairway to Heaven • Take the Long Way Home • and more.

00196019 Piano Solo $14.99

CHRISTMAS CAROLS

Away in a Manger • Deck the Hall • The First Noel • God Rest Ye Merry, Gentlemen • Hark! the Herald Angels Sing • It Came upon the Midnight Clear • Jingle Bells • Joy to the World • O Holy Night • Silent Night • Up on the Housetop • We Three Kings of Orient Are • What Child Is This? • and more.

00147214 Piano Solo $14.99

CHRISTMAS COLLECTION

Blue Christmas • The Christmas Song (Chestnuts Roasting on an Open Fire) • Frosty the Snow Man • Here Comes Santa Claus (Right down Santa Claus Lane) • Let It Snow! Let It Snow! Let It Snow! • Silver Bells • Sleigh Ride • White Christmas • Winter Wonderland • and more.

00172042 Piano Solo $14.99

CLASSIC ROCK

Another One Bites the Dust • Aqualung • Beast of Burden • Born to Be Wild • Carry on Wayward Son • Layla • Owner of a Lonely Heart • Roxanne • Smoke on the Water • Sweet Emotion • Takin' It to the Streets • 25 or 6 to 4 • Welcome to the Jungle • and more!

00138517 Piano Solo $14.99

Prices, contents, and availability subject to change without notice.

DISNEY FAVORITES

Beauty and the Beast • Can You Feel the Love Tonight • Chim Chim Cher-ee • For the First Time in Forever • How Far I'll Go • Let It Go • Mickey Mouse March • Remember Me (Ernesto de la Cruz) • You'll Be in My Heart • You've Got a Friend in Me • and more.

00283318 Piano Solo $14.99

JAZZ POP SONGS

Don't Know Why • I Just Called to Say I Love You • I Put a Spell on You • Just the Way You Are • Killing Me Softly with His Song • Mack the Knife • Michelle • Smooth Operator • Sunny • Take Five • What a Wonderful World • and more.

00195426 Piano Solo $14.99

JAZZ STANDARDS

All the Things You Are • Beyond the Sea • Georgia on My Mind • In the Wee Small Hours of the Morning • The Lady Is a Tramp • Like Someone in Love • A Nightingale Sang in Berkeley Square • Someone to Watch Over Me • That's All • What'll I Do? • and more.

00283317 Piano Solo $14.99

POP BALLADS

Against All Odds (Take a Look at Me Now) • Bridge over Troubled Water • Fields of Gold • Hello • I Want to Know What Love Is • Imagine • In Your Eyes • Let It Be • She's Got a Way • Total Eclipse of the Heart • You Are So Beautiful • Your Song • and more.

00195425 Piano Solo $14.99

POP HITS

Billie Jean • Fields of Gold • Get Lucky • Happy • Ho Hey • I'm Yours • Just the Way You Are • Let It Go • Poker Face • Radioactive • Roar • Rolling in the Deep • Royals • Smells like Teen Spirit • Viva la Vida • Wonderwall • and more.

00138156 Piano Solo $14.99

www.halleonard.com